INDIAN CHARTERS ON COPPER PLATES

IN THE DEPARTMENT OF ORIENTAL MANUSCRIPTS AND PRINTED BOOKS

BY

ALBERTINE GAUR

PUBLISHED FOR
THE BRITISH LIBRARY
BY
BRITISH MUSEUM PUBLICATIONS LIMITED

ISBN 0 7141 0650 X

Published by
British Museum Publications Limited
6 Bedford Square
London WC1B 3RA

Set in 11 on 13 point Imprint and
Printed in Great Britain
at the University Press, Oxford
by Vivian Ridler
Printer to the University

CONTENTS

PLATES

PREFACE

THE sixty-seven Charters described in this Catalogue, some of which are nearly 2000 years old, are in various languages of North and South India, except for one, in Javanese, which may be said to belong to Indonesia's Hindu heritage. All of them except eleven have been previously mentioned in journals, especially in *Epigraphia Indica* and *The Indian Antiquary*, and Dr Albertine Gaur has made full use of such work already done. Most of her entries contain references to relevant articles by L. D. Barnett, J. F. Fleet, and others. But in bringing this scattered material together for the first time she has supplemented the information and judgements of her predecessors with the results of her own research and direct experience of India. She also quotes the opinions of eminent Hindu scholars who have visited the Department during the last ten years.

MARTIN LINGS
*Keeper of Oriental Manuscripts
and Printed Books*

INTRODUCTION

ROYAL charters (*Rāja-śāsanas*) engraved on copper plates are already mentioned in some of the early Indian law books.[1] They usually refer to revenue-free land granted by a king or subordinate ruler in favour of persons (mostly Brahmins), deities, or religious establishments. These copper plates, often bearing the seal of the donor, served the donee as title-deeds, proving for all time and for the benefit of his descendants his claim to the property. Since donation of land was an act designed to win religious merit the number of copper plates issued since the beginning of the Christian era must have been considerable. At times we even come across passages where a poet, praising the unrivalled generosity of his patron, speaks of a shortage of copper[2] as a direct result of the king's liberal grants of land. Though this is no doubt poetic exaggeration (the poet was probably hoping for a similar grant) it throws an interesting light on the typically Indian attitude which makes generosity more or less compulsory for the privileged classes. The desire to issue as many land grants as possible did indeed sometimes go so far as to make a ruler disguise the sale of land as a gift, or claim credit for a donation which had been made by somebody of inferior rank during the king's reign. *Ind. Ch.* 55, for example, records plainly the sale of land. Although L. D. Barnett has thrown some doubt on the authenticity of this particular charter, copper plates recording the sale of land, either openly[3] or in a disguised fashion (the donee is expected to render money or services in exchange for the grant, he has in fact to pay revenue for the 'gift',[4] etc.), are known to exist. These, however, were no doubt exceptions.

Copper plates were valuable documents and as such carefully preserved by the donee and his descendants. If lost, the revenue-free

[1] *According to Viṣṇu* '... [the King] should grant land to Brahmaṇas. For the information of future kings, he should also give the donee of the grant a charter written on cloth or copper-plate endowed with his own seal and with a description of the boundaries of the land, of his ancestors and of the measurement of the area. He should not confiscate land granted by others ... The king should kill persons who prepare spurious charters, and also those preparing spurious documents ...', ch. 3, vv 81–2; ch. 5, vv 9–10, and vol. v, pp. 9–10.

[2] Ballāla's *Bhojaprabhanda* (Nirnayasagara Press, 1932), p. 34, verse 162.

[3] *Journal of the Andhra Historical Research Society* (Rajahmundry), vol. viii, p. 180, and *Journal of the Royal Asiatic Society* (London), 1952, p. 4.

[4] *Epigraphia Indica*, vol. xxx, pp. 114–15; ibid., vol. xxxiii, p. 150; ibid., vol. xxxiv, p. 140.

holdings created by them could again relapse into ordinary rent-paying land. Occasionally, when charters were destroyed by fire or other calamities beyond human control, they were officially reissued.[1] Monks living in artificial caves would sometimes engrave the texts of copper-plate grants on the walls as an additional insurance.[2] A large number of copper plates have been found immured in walls or foundations of houses belonging to the families of donees or hidden in small caches made of bricks or stone in the fields to which the grant refers.[3] Sometimes several plates were kept hidden together (see *Ind. Ch. 58–Ind. Ch. 64*), and plates have been found far away from their place of issue, which probably meant that the descendants of the original donee had left their old home.

Copper-plate charters come from all over India. They are written in a variety of Indian languages and scripts and show considerable difference in shape and size. Some are rectangular[4] with angular or rounded edges, others resemble stone stelae,[5] and some grants were even written on axe-heads. The most popular variety, however, are plates of smaller size resembling palmyra leaves or bark sheets. This resemblance is not entirely accidental. According to literary sources, the texts were at first often written on perishable material like birch bark or palmyra leaf before they were copied on to copper. At times the text was written with ink directly on to the plate for the engraver to follow, and the quality of the engraving varies considerably. Influential rulers presiding over powerful courts usually had well-trained and competent engravers in their service, but plates issued by private individuals[6] or minor chieftains[7] are often full of errors apart from the poor quality of the actual engraving. In the case of some early charters the letters are formed by a series of dots instead of continuous lines,[8] and a number of early

[1] See, for example, the Kurud plates of Narēndra. *Epigraphia Indica*, vol. xxxi, p. 267.

[2] *Proceedings of the Historical Records Commission*, Lahore, 1940, p. 54. Such inscriptions have been found from the second century A.D. onwards, which means that the custom of engraving grants on copper plates was already well established at that time. See also *Select Inscriptions bearing on Indian History and Civilisation*, pp. 157, 191, 193. We have many instances where royal grants were copied on temple walls or stone slabs: see *Epigraphia Indica*, vol. vi, p. 89; vol. xiii, pp. 15, 16, 27.

[3] G. Bühler, *Indian Palaeography*, pp. 99–100.

[4] *Epigraphia Indica*, vol. xxix, p. 168 and plates between pp. 40 and 41. Ibid. vol. xxxi, plates between pp. 306 and 307.

[5] Ibid., vol. xiv, plates between pp. 348 and 349.

[6] Ibid., vol. xxviii, p. 44. According to the *Mitākṣarā* on the *Yājñavalkyasmṛti* (ii. 89) a royal deed had to be written in correct and elegant language, although documents of ordinary people were not required to be written in correct Sanskrit and could even be written in the local dialect.

[7] *Epigraphia Indica*, vol. xxviii, pp. 112, 276, 290, 324.

[8] Ibid., vol. iv, p. 54; ibid., vol. xxi, plate facing p. 259.

South Indian copper plates have extremely shallow engraving. Some scholars believe that the letters may have been scratched into the surface of the plate with a sharp instrument (as a stylus is used on the palmyra leaf) while the plates were covered with a layer of mud.[1] The position of the scribe and the engraver seems to have been of considerable importance and proper manuals exist for the guidance of clerks who prepared land grants and similar documents at court.[2] Single plates are usually quite thick, large, and have a seal affixed to the left or the top of the margin. Records written on more than one plate are smaller in size and held together by a copper ring which has the seal soldered to its joint (three was the most popular number though one existing Cōṟa grant is written on as many as fifty-five plates).[3] Bigger plates of later periods often have slightly raised rims in order to avoid any friction which might have damaged the script. Another method of protecting the text consisted of riveting copper bands on to the margin of the inscribed side of each plate. The seal—in bronze or copper—usually has a countersunk surface decorated with the royal emblem, the legend, the donor's name, and/or various devices such as the sun and the moon (to indicate that the grant should last as long as sun and moon endured),[4] a lotus, lamp-stands, cowries, and auspicious symbols or religious emblems indicative of the donor's spiritual affinities. Some of the royal seals are quite large and heavy and elaborately decorated. Most charters described in this Catalogue have a cut ring. This may mean that at one time an ink rubbing had been taken for scholarly purposes, but it can also indicate that somebody had tampered with the plates. Indeed, six of the present charters (i.e. *Ind. Ch. 5*; *Ind. Ch. 9*; *Ind. Ch. 19*; *Ind. Ch. 46*; *Ind. Ch. 56*; and *Ind. Ch. 66*) are probably ancient forgeries. Old, rejected plates were sometimes quite legitimately used to prepare new charters. In most cases they were melted down to form a new sheet from which smaller plates could be cut. The old writing was then completely lost, only traces of hammering are sometimes noticeable on such plates. But, quite often, the original inscription was merely beaten out with a hammer and the new text written over the erasure,[5] leaving a good deal of the original inscription still visible. The first plate of *Ind. Ch. 12*, for example, bears traces of an inscription

[1] *Epigraphia Indica*, vol. xxvii, plates between pp. 128, 129, 130, 131.

[2] G. Bühler, *Indian Palaeography*, p. 102.

[3] This is the Karandai inscription from the 8th regnal year of the Cōṟa Rajēndra I (A.D. 1016–1043): see *Journal of Oriental Research* (Madras), vol. xix, p. 148.

[4] *Epigraphia Indica*, vol. xxxii, plate between pp. 168 and 169.

[5] Ibid., vol. xxv, plate facing p. 191; ibid., vol. xxiii, plate facing p. 106.

which may refer to the names of the original donees. Doubts have been cast on the authenticity of *Ind. Ch. 54* and *Ind. Ch. 66* but the plates may well be genuine. *Ind. Ch. 13* recording—in Sanskrit—a grant made by the *Mahārājādhirāja* Arivarman [Harivarman] has often been called a forgery but is probably perfectly authentic. The grant is dated *Śaka-samvat* 169 [i.e. A.D. 247/8] and if genuine would be the earliest existing copper-plate charter; a place so far held by the Prakrit charters of the Pallava kings of Kanchi and the Mayidavolu and Hirahadagaddi plates of Śivaskandavarman, both assigned to the middle of the fourth century A.D.[1]

The text of most charters can be divided into three basic sections: introduction, notification, and conclusion. Grants from different historical periods, different geographical areas, and different rulers may show alterations or omissions but the pattern is usually the same. The introductory section of the grant opens with an invocation which can vary from a single word (like *siddham*,[2] *svasti*, *Om*) to a lengthy passage in verse and prose in honour of the grantor's favourite deities. Some medieval copper plates may also bear the representation of the royal crest instead of a seal.[3] Then follows the name of the place where the grant was issued. Since grants were usually issued in the capital of the donor the place-name may well be omitted because it was taken for granted that everybody knew about it. But a royal camp—in the case of a military expedition—or a place of pilgrimage, may equally well have served suitably for issuing a grant. The most important part of the introduction is the portion which deals with the name of the donor, his royal titles, his ancestry, sometimes even his military conquests or descriptions of other grants, especially if made to religious establishments. In the case of later grants this part is often extremely long and elaborate and as such a useful source of information for the historian. Whole genealogies have been pieced together solely on the basis of various copper-plate grants. Since, as a whole, Indians lack the sharp historical sense which, for example, distinguishes the Arabs the value of those charters can hardly be overestimated. The portion related to the donor is often couched in most poetic and extravagant terms. Legendary and factual history, the actual deeds of the king and the description of his real or (one is sometimes tempted to think) imaginary personal charms and

[1] D. C. Sircar, *Select Inscriptions bearing on Indian History and Civilisation*, pp. 433, 437. D. C. Sircar, *The Successors of the Sātavāhanas in the Lower Deccan*, p. 165.

[2] D. C. Sircar, *Select Inscriptions bearing on Indian History and Civilisation*, pp. 157, 160, 164, 165, 169, 176, 191, 193, 196, 200, 203, 205.

[3] *Epigraphia Indica*, vol. xxxi, p. 72; ibid., vol. xxxii, plate facing p. 156.

qualities, are closely intermingled. A typical example can be found in *Ind. Ch. 43* where the donor is described as '. . . the devotee of Maheś-vara, the illustrious *Mahārāja* Guhasena, who proved his courage by splitting the temples of the rutting elephants of his enemies, the rays of whose footnails mingle with the glitter of the crest jewels of his enemies who are prostrated before him in consequence of his power, who gives its proper significance to the title *rāja* (winner of hearts) since he won the hearts of his subjects by carefully keeping to the path prescribed in the *Smṛtis*, who in beauty surpasses the [god of love], in splendour the moon, in firmness the Lord of mountains, in depth the ocean, in wisdom the protector of the gods, in riches the Lord of Wealth,—who, intent on affording safety to those seeking refuge with him, cares not a straw for his own interest,—who rejoicing the hearts of the learned and of his affectionate friends by granting them more wealth than their prayers demand,—who is as it were the incarnate delight of the whole world . . .'[1] The introductory part of the grant ends with an address to subordinates, officials or to the inhabitants of the area where the village or land described in the grant is situated.

The notification, the central part of the grant, consists basically of a specification of the gift, the name of the donee, the occasion when the grant was made, its specific purpose, and a description of the boundaries of the gift land. These four items may not always appear in exactly the same order. Sometimes certain parts are altogether missing.

The gift might range from one relatively small plot of land to several villages, just as the donee might be one person or, as in the case of a grant made by Rājendra Cōṟa I, as many as 1073 Brahmins.[2] The grant was not always given outright to a person or a religious institution. Its use and purpose is often specifically mentioned, as in *Ind. Ch. 63* which states '. . . for the purpose of providing annually, at the great eight-day sacrifice, the perpetual anointing with clarified butter for the temple of the *Arhat* which Mṛgēśa, the son of the General Siṅha of the lineage of *Bhāradvāja*, had caused to be built at Palāśikā, and that whatever might remain over after this was to be devoted to the purpose of feeding the whole sect . . .', or, more straightforward in *Ind. Ch. 65*, a village was given to a Brahmin '. . . in order to provide for oblations, incense and lamps for the goddess . . .'. The majority of grants mention that the gift was made at the occasion of an eclipse of the sun or the moon (this offers the historian a means for checking the authenticity of certain

[1] *Indian Antiquary*, vol. iv, p. 175.
[2] *Journal of Oriental Research* (Madras), vol. xix, p. 148.

grants), a religious festival, a visit to a sacred temple, or simply after the donor had taken a ceremonial bath in the waters of a holy river.[1] The purpose of the grant—usually the accumulation of religious merit in favour of the donor and his family—is frequently mentioned. Sometimes the grant was made at the request of the donor's wife, mother, sister, his parents, an official of his court, or some subordinate ruler. In *Ind. Ch. 24* a village was given to a Jain teacher at the request of a certain lady called Chāmekāmbā who seems to have been a professional courtesan and one of the king's mistresses. In cases where the boundaries of the grant were locally well known they are often only vaguely defined, but in other cases great care is taken to make sure that the gift land could not be violated either by ignorance or by pleading ignorance of its actual boundaries.

The concluding part of the charter begins with a stern request on the part of the donor to respect the gift. This request is addressed to all present and future kings of his own or any other lineage. Those who fail to obey are threatened with 60,000 years in hell and a never-ending rebirth (see *Ind. Ch. 60*), or guilty of the sin of slaughtering a thousand cows at Vārāṇasī.[2] However, those who respect the grant can hope for high rewards; thus a passage in *Ind. Ch. 62* states that the '. . . king who, from envy or negligence or even avarice, injures those (*nivartanas*), his family shall be plunged into hell and shall not escape from it up to the seventh generation; but he whether born in his own lineage or in the lineage of another, who, being desirous of acquiring religious merits, preserves them, shall disport himself for a long time in heaven with the lovely women of the gods . . .' Usually a grant ends with the name of the official responsible for the preparation of the document and the date when the grant was made. The date (missing in some charters) may either be given in great detail or just mentioned by referring to the year of the king's rule in which the grant was made.

Copper plates (as indeed most epigraphic data) are usually dated according to regnal reckoning or according to a particular era. The month, fortnight, and day are sometimes mentioned (especially in later charters) and occasionally additional details such as the *nakṣatra*, etc., are added. The date of the actual grant is sometimes earlier than that of the issue of the plates,[3] and the year quoted may be current or expired, just as it is not always certain whether the regnal years of a king

[1] *Epigraphia Indica*, vol. xxix, p. 8, text line 46.
[2] Ibid., vol. xxxii, p. 174.
[3] Ibid., vol. xvii, p. 337.

were counted exactly from the date of his accession or whether they were adjusted with the regular years of the almanac. Added to this, the competence of the astrologer who worked out the date is an important factor as to its reliability. (Sometimes a court astrologer had reasons to fabricate a cosmic moment—such as an eclipse of the sun—to add further justification and weight to the issue of a grant.) The earliest documents of Indian kings do not refer to eras but only to regnal years. In the case of some dynasties, like the Guptas or the dynasty of Vikramāditya (*Vikrama-samvat*), this regnal reckoning led eventually to the establishment of proper eras. The majority of the sixty-seven charters discussed in this Catalogue are dated in the *Vikrama* or the *Śaka* era. *Vikrama-samvat* begins in 58 B.C., *Śaka-samvat* in A.D. 78/9. These are the two most popular ancient Indian systems of dating. *Samvat* originally only meant 'year' but in the course of time it began to stand for 'era'. In some of the later, unedited plates (see *Ind. Ch. 18* or *Ind. Ch. 33*) L. D. Barnett (in some of his notes) has translated *Samvat* simply as belonging to the *Vikrama* era which is probably perfectly justified. Other, less well-known eras mentioned in the Catalogue are the *Cēdi* era and the *Valabhī-Gupta* era. The *Cēdi* date[1] of reckoning was first used by the Kalacuris who ruled over the ancient Cedi country with Tripuri as their capital. The first inscription bearing this date comes from the Konkan and belongs to the middle of the fifth century A.D. Its use does not seem to have spread far beyond the sphere of influence of the Kalacuris and after the fall of this dynasty in the thirteenth century it went out of use altogether. The *Cēdi* era is generally thought to begin about A.D. 248/9, although there are discrepancies in various inscriptions. The *Valabhī-Gupta* era is believed to begin in A.D. 319 but this date too is not accepted by everyone.

The sixty-seven charters come from various parts of India. They are written in Sanskrit, [Old]-Kannada, Prakrit, Tamil, [Old]-Telugu, Hindi, Gujarati, a mixed dialect of Hindi and Gujarati and in Rajasthani. One charter comes from South-East Asia and is written in Javanese. The scripts used are *Grantha*, *Nagārī*, Tamil, *Vaṭṭeṟuttu*, Old-Kannada, *Nandināgarī*, and *Devanāgarī*. The dynasties or royal houses to which the grantors belonged were those of the Pallavas, the Pāṇḍyas, Eastern Cāḷukyas, Western Cāḷukyas, Raṣṭrakūṭas, Gaṅgas, Sēndrakas, Gurjaras, the Reḍḍi kings of Rajahmundry, Cēdi rulers, Kanauj kings, Śilāhāras, Dēvagiri-Yādava kings, the Kadambas and the kings of Karṇāṭa, the successors of the kings of Vijayanagar. They were either Hindus,

[1] *Indian Antiquary*, vol. xx, p. 84; ibid., vol. xxii, p. 82.

Buddhists, or Jains. Eleven of the grants (*Ind. Ch. 18*; *Ind. Ch. 39*; *Ind. Ch. 40*; *Ind. Ch. 41*; *Ind. Ch. 45*; *Ind. Ch. 50*; *Ind. Ch. 51*; *Ind. Ch. 55*; *Ind. Ch. 56*; *Ind. Ch. 66*; and *Ind. Ch.* 67) have not yet been properly edited. The majority of the unedited plates are as late as the nineteenth century and therefore of limited importance, except for *Ind. Ch. 55* which, dated in *Kali-yuga*, seems to belong to the fifteenth century and is written in Tamil. *Ind. Ch. 66* comes from the seventh century and *Ind. Ch. 67* consists of seven miscellaneous plates with incomplete texts, all from the eighth century, written in *Grantha* and rather badly damaged. Some of the grants were edited before the plates came into the possession of the Museum and anybody coming by chance across an article discussing them (usually either in the *Indian Antiquary* or the *Epigraphia Indica*) might well have wondered what had become of them. Copper-plate charters often have a quite adventurous history. *Ind. Ch. 1*, for example, was first discussed by B. Gangdhara Shastri in a very superficial manner in 1844. After this the plates disappeared completely until they suddenly turned up in a London auction room in 1884 where A. W. Franks bought them and presented them to the Museum.[1] Some of the plates might greatly benefit from a re-editing of the text as much epigraphic evidence has come to light since the end of the last century.

The majority of the charters (*Ind. Ch. 2–Ind. Ch. 15* and *Ind. Ch. 21–Ind. Ch. 32*) were presented to the Museum by Sir Walter Elliot in 1887. *Ind. Ch. 1* and *Ind. Ch. 44–Ind. Ch. 46* were presented by Sir Augustus Wollaston Franks. The *Mahārāja* Venkates Raman Prasad Singh of Rewah presented *Ind. Ch. 34–Ind. Ch. 41* to the Museum in 1889, using for this purpose the offices of Major D. W. K. Barr, Political Agent in Rewah. J. F. Fleet presented *Ind. Ch. 42* and in 1917, after his death, *Ind. Ch. 58–Ind. Ch. 64* reached the collection of the Department by bequest. *Ind. Ch. 50* and *Ind. Ch. 51* were presented by a Mrs Steuart and *Ind. Ch. 65* was the gift of A. Scott Napier. The Museum purchased *Ind. Ch. 43* from Mr William Payne; *Ind. Ch. 16* from Lieut.-Colonel H. Szczepanski (10 July 1886); *Ind. Ch. 17* and *Ind. Ch. 18* from Mr Archibald Carlleyle (23 November 1887); *Ind. Ch. 19* and *Ind. Ch. 20* from Dr G. Bühler; *Ind. Ch. 48* and *Ind. Ch. 49* from Colonel G. H. Hall (in 1911); and *Ind. Ch. 52* from E. W. Martindell. *Ind. Ch. 47* seems to have been presented by Mr James Burgess. *Ind. Ch. 57* comes from the Stamford Raffles Collection (Singapore) and *Ind. Ch. 66* reached the Museum via Miss C. M. Newton, although

[1] *Indian Antiquary*, vol. xix, pp. 303–11.

it is uncertain whether by donation or purchase. There are no records about the original ownership of *Ind. Ch. 33*; *Ind. Ch. 53*; *Ind. Ch. 54*; *Ind. Ch. 55*; *Ind. Ch. 56*; and *Ind. Ch. 66*; nor about the miscellaneous collection of charters listed under *Ind. Ch.* 67.

London, July 1971

THE CHARTERS

IND. CH. 1

Three copper plates (17·5×8 cm.) held together by a cut copper ring with a circular seal (2 cm. diameter). The countersunk surface of the seal bears, written across the centre, the legend *Śrī Biṭṭarasa* (i.e. the illustrious king Biṭṭi or Biṭṭa). Underneath a boar, facing to the proper right, is squatting on his haunches. Above the inscription appears a representation of the moon.

The grant is written in Sanskrit. It was made in the eighth year of the reign of the *Mahārāja* (scil. the Western Cāḷukya Pulakēsin II) by the *Yuvarāja* Viṣṇuvardhana I [also called Viṣamasiddhi], the founder of the Eastern branch of the Cāḷukya family. The inscription records that in *Śaka-samvat* 539/40 (i.e. A.D. 616/17) '. . . for the acquisition of religious merit by his parents and by himself, on the full-moon *tithi* of the month *Kārttika* there had been given, with libations of water according to due rite, the village named Alandatīrtha, in the Śrīnilaya *bhōga*, on the north of the *agrāhāra* of Aṇopalya and on the south bank of the river Bhīmarathī, to the sons of Lakṣmaṇasvāmin . . . for the maintainance of the great five sacrifices . . .'. The plates were found at Satara.

J. F. Fleet, 'Sanskrit and Old-Canarese Inscriptions', in *The Indian Antiquary*, vol. xix, pp. 303–11. Bāl Gangādhar Śāstri, *Journal of the Bombay Branch of the Royal Asiatic Society*, vol. ii (1844). [This article gives the first, rather inadequate publication of the grant.] *Epigraphia Indica*, vol. vii, App. no. 547 (p. 92).

IND. CH. 2

Three copper plates (15×5 cm.) held together by a cut copper ring with a circular seal (3 cm. diameter). Sunk into the surface of the seal is the figure of an animal described by Fleet as a deer which, however, looks more like a long-horned humped bull. The inscription is in Prakrit and records a grant made to the god Nārāyaṇa by the Queen consort of the *Yuvamahārāja* Vijayabuddhavarmā in the reign of the *Mahārāja* Vijayaskandavarmā. The copper plates were found in the Guntur district. No date is given but they are obviously the record of an early Pallava grant.

J. F. Fleet, 'Sanskrit and Old-Canarese Inscriptions', in *The Indian Antiquary*, vol. ix, pp. 100–1. *Epigraphia Indica*, vol. vii, App. no. 616 (p. 106).

IND. CH. 3

Three copper plates (23×4 cm.) held together by a cut copper ring with a circular seal (2 cm. diameter). An emblem has been scratched into the flat surface of the seal which Fleet interpreted as a god sitting cross-legged on an altar. The third plate, now blank, shows traces of a carefully beaten-out inscription.

The language of the grant is Sanskrit and it records how the *Rājā* Attivarmā of the race of king Kandara gave the village of Anturkkūr, and a field measuring eight hundred *paṭṭis* (or a field called *Aṣṭaśata-paṭṭi*) at the village of Tānthikontha on the south bank of the river Kṛṣṇabeṇṇā to a Brahmin named Koṭṭiśarmā. The grant is not dated but belongs apparently to an early period of the Pallava dynasty.

The plates were found in Gorantla in the Guntur district.

J. F. Fleet, 'Sanskrit and Old-Canarese Inscriptions', in *The Indian Antiquary*, vol. ix, pp. 102–3. *Epigraphia Indica*, vol. vii, App. no. 1015 (p. 162).

IND. CH. 4

Ten copper plates (27·5×8 cm.) held together by a thin, cut copper ring without a seal. The grant is written partly in Sanskrit in the *Grantha* script (lines 1–30 and lines 142–50), and partly in Tamil using *Vaṭṭeṟuttu* characters (lines 31–141 and 151–5). Sanskrit words occurring in Tamil passages are also written in *Grantha*, but their spelling is often influenced by Tamil rules of orthography. The plates are numbered with *Grantha* letter symbols.

This grant is of special historical interest. The Sanskrit portion begins with an invocation of the god Śiva, followed by tales related to the Pāṇḍya lineage. The Tamil part contains the actual grant. It describes how the Pāṇḍya king Palyāgamudukuḍumi Peruvaṟudi gave the village Vēḷvikuḍi (i.e. the village of sacrifice) to Naṟkoṟṟaṉ, the headman of Koṟkai, in appreciation of a Vedic sacrifice performed by the latter. Then follows a historical narration, describing how the country was conquered by enemies and reconquered by the Pāṇḍyas. After many battles king Parāntaka Neḍuñjaḍaiyaṉ succeeded in re-establishing a more permanent peace. '. . . while the third year of the reign of this king was current, one day a bystander of Kūḍal [i.e. Madurai], the city of mansions and high ramparts, having cried out by way of complaint the king at once called him mildly and was pleased to ask him first: "What is your complaint?" The bystander submitted thus: "Oh mighty king of powerful army. Formerly without swerving from the pure path prescribed by law, the village called Vēḷvikuḍi included in Pāgaṉūr-kūṟṟam, whose flowery groves touched the sky, was designated Vēḷvi-kuḍi . . . was granted through the *Kēḷvi* [Brahmins] by your ancestor, the great lord known as Palyāgamudukuḍumi Peruvaṟudi, who protected the earth girt by the ocean with an army of spearmen who never

Ind. Ch. 4. Example of Vaṭṭeṟuttu script

missed. It has since been resumed by the ignoble yet ocean-like army of the Kaḷabhras." The king gently smiled and said: "Very well, very well, prove the antiquity of the gift by a reference to the district assembly and receive it back." He proved then and there the antiquity of his claim . . . Thereupon the powerful king of long arms holding the bow, being overjoyed was pleased to declare: "What was granted by my ancestors according to rule, is also granted by Us." And saying so, he of many chariots and ocean-like army, gave it with libations of water to Kāmak-kāṇi Naṟchiṅgaṉ, the headman of Koṟkai . . .' (lines 103–17). The composer of the Tamil portion was the *Sēnāpati* Ēnādi alias Cāttaṉ Cāttaṉ, the engraver's name was Yuddhakēsari Perumbaṇaikkāraṉ. The engraving was ordered by the king himself.

The ten plates of the Vēḷvikuḍi grant were found at Madakulam. There is some controversy about the actual date of the grant but according to historical evidence it was probably made in A.D. 769/70.

H. Krishna Shastri, 'Velvikudi Grant of Nedunjadaiyan: the Third Year of his Reign', in *Epigraphia Indica*, vol. xvii, pp. 291–309. K. G. Shankara, 'The Velvikudi Plates of Jatila Parantakar' (*c.* A.D. 770), in *Quarterly Journal of the Mythic Society* (Bangalore), vol. xiii, no. 1, pp. 448–58. *Progress Report of the Assistant Archaeological Superintendent for Epigraphy, Southern Circle*, 1906–7, p. 62, and 1907–8, p. 62. Robert Sewell, *The Historical Inscriptions of Southern India* (Madras) 1932, p. 30.

IND. CH. 5

Two thick copper plates (30×14·5 cm.) with raised rims, showing minor damages and repairs. The text is incomplete; originally a third plate, now missing, may have been added to the grant. The two existing plates are held together by a cut copper ring with square seal (4×4·5 cm.). The seal shows a representation of the moon and the sun and underneath a boar facing to the proper left.

The grant is probably a forgery. It claims to have been made by the Western Cāḷukya Vikramāditya I and gives the date *Śaka-samvat* 532 (i.e. A.D. 610). Both the language and orthography of the grant are full of mistakes. The characters are fully developed Old Kannada characters of the ninth or tenth century, though attempts have occasionally been made to imitate more ancient forms.

J. F. Fleet, 'Sanskrit and Old Canarese Inscriptions', in *The Indian Antiquary*, vol. vii, pp. 217–20. A. C. Burnell, *Elements of South Indian Palaeography*, revised edition, Delhi, 1968, p. 87, plate xxii. Walter Elliot, *Journal Madras Branch of the Royal Asiatic Society*, vol. vii, p. 199. Unlike Fleet and Barnett, Burnell and Elliot seem to accept the authenticity of the grant. Burnell and Elliot date the grant *Śaka-samvat* 530 (i.e. A.D. 608)

IND. CH. 6

Seven copper plates (20×5·5 cm.) held together by a cut copper ring with an oval seal (4×0·75 cm.). The seal shows a representation of the moon, written across the centre the legend *Śrī Viṣamasiddhi*, and below it a lotus. The language of the grant is Sanskrit, rather ungrammatical in places, and the characters are of the early Eastern Cāḷukya type. All seven plates are well preserved.

The grant was made by the Eastern Cāḷukya *Mahārāja* Viṣṇuvardhana II, a grandson of Viṣṇuvardhana I, on the '. . . 10th day of the bright fortnight of the month *Caitra* under the *Maghā-nakṣatra* . . .' in the second year of the king's reign. J. F. Fleet has equated this date with *Śaka-samvat* 590 (i.e. A.D. 668/9) whereas L. D. Barnett comes to the conclusion that the grant was made on 13 March, A.D. 664. The grant describes the division of the village of Reyūru which, at the king's order, was given to a number of different people.

J. F. Fleet, 'Sanskrit and Old-Canarese Inscriptions', in *The Indian Antiquary*, vol. vii, pp. 186–92, and vol. viii, p. 320 (plates). *Epigraphia Indica*, vol. vii, App. no. 550 (p. 93).

IND. CH. 7

Two copper plates (16×5 cm.) held together by a cut copper ring with a circular seal (4·5 cm. diameter). The seal shows, in relief, at the top the moon, in the middle the legend *Śrī Viṣamasiddhi*, and below a lotus.

The language is Sanskrit, and the characters are of the usual Eastern Cāḷukya type. The two plates form the beginning of a grant made by the Eastern Cāḷukya *Mahārāja* Viṣṇuvardhana II. It is addressed to '. . . all who reside at the village of Paḷḷivāḍa in the district of Gudrahāra in the vicinity of Aṟutaṅkūr . . .', informing them that '. . . at this village in the fifth year of Our victorious reign in the month of *Phālguṇa*, on the day of the new-moon, on account of an eclipse of the sun there has been given to Dhruvaśarmā, who has studied two *Vedas*, the son's son of Dhruvaśarmā who inhabited the city of Asanapura . . .'. After some further reference to the person of the donee the grant breaks off. J. F. Fleet translated the date into *Śaka-samvat* 581 (i.e. A.D. 659/60), whereas L. D. Barnett gave 17 February, A.D. 668 as a possible date.

J. F. Fleet, 'Sanskrit and Old-Canarese Inscriptions', in *The Indian Antiquary*, vol. vii, pp. 191–2. *Epigraphia Indica*, vol. vii, App. no. 551 (p. 93).

IND. CH. 8

Five copper plates (18·5×9·5 cm.) held together by a cut copper ring with a round seal (6 cm. diameter). The top of the seal shows representations of the sun and the moon; below it are a boar facing to the proper left and an elephant-goad. The legend *Śrī Tribhuvanāṁkuśa* (i.e. the elephant-goad of Śrī Tribhuvanan) is written across the centre of the seal. The lowest part of the seal is decorated by an open lotus.

The grant is written in Sanskrit. It begins with the usual invocations, followed by a reference to the lineage of the Eastern Cāḷukyas. The donee's name is given as Paṇḍiya, a Brahmin of the Bhāradvāja *gotra* '. . . worthy to be prescribed as an example for good people, possessing a personal appearance that was commended, having an undisturbed mind, pure, versed in the three *Vedas*, and resolute in investigating proper behaviour. To him, the religious student, the pilgrim, who has devoted himself to conciliating my feet, the village named Paḍaṁkalūru . . . has been given by Us on the occasion of an eclipse of the moon . . .'. The grantor is the Eastern Cāḷukya *Mahārājādhirāja* Ammarāja II, also called Vijayāditya VI. The grant was made in *Śaka-samvat* 867 which L. D. Barnett translated into 5 December, A.D. 945.

J. F. Fleet, 'Sanskrit and Old-Canarese Inscriptions', in *The Indian Antiquary*, vol. vii, pp. 15–16. A. C. Burnell, *Elements of South Indian Palaeography*, plate xxv. *Epigraphia Indica*, vol. vii, App. no. 563 (p. 95).

IND. CH. 9

Five copper plates (22 × 7 cm.) with raised rims held together by a cut copper ring. One plate is without inscription. The orthography of the grant is rather inaccurate. Up to line seventeen the language is Sanskrit. The rest is written in Old-Telugu. The grant records the gift of the village of Pṛthivippallavapaṭṭana by the Eastern Cāḷukya *Mahārāja* Viṣṇuvardhana V, son of Vijayāditya II and grandson of Viṣṇuvardhana IV. No date is given and the grant itself is of dubious authenticity.

The plates were found at Ahadanakaram, Madras Presidency.

J. F. Fleet, 'Sanskrit and Old-Canarese Inscriptions', in *The Indian Antiquary*, vol. xiii, pp. 185–7. *Epigraphia Indica*, vol. vii, App. no. 555 (p. 94).

IND. CH. 10

Three copper plates (20·5 × 9 cm.) with raised rims held together by a copper ring with a circular seal (6·5 cm. diameter). The ring is now cut but was apparently still intact when Fleet examined the plates. The seal shows, in relief on a countersunk surface, the legend *Śrī Tribhuvanāṁkuśa* written across the centre. Above it is a representation of the moon, below it a standing boar facing to the proper right and a lotus. Fleet speaks of 'the sun and the moon' but it is difficult to distinguish anything that could be identified as a representation of the sun. The plates seem to have suffered considerable damage in the last hundred years.

The language of the grant is Sanskrit. The grant was made by the Eastern Cāḷukya *Mahārājādhirāja* Ammarāja II, also called Vijayāditya VI, at the request of his wife's parents Kāma and Nāyamāmbā. It records the gift of a field at the village of Guṇḍugolanu, in the *viṣaya* of Veṅgī (or Veṅgīnāṇḍu), to a Brahmin named Vāmanaśarmā of the Bhāradvāja *gotra*, who was an inhabitant of the village of Kallūru. No date is given.

J. F. Fleet, 'Sanskrit and Old-Canarese Inscriptions', in *The Indian Antiquary*, vol. xiii, pp. 248–50. *Epigraphia Indica*, vol. vii, App. no. 566 (p. 96).

IND. CH. 11

Three copper plates (14·5×6·5 cm.) held together by a cut copper ring with a circular seal (3·5 cm. diameter). The seal shows, in relief on a countersunk surface, the god Śiva sitting with bent knees so that the soles of his feet touch each other, holding a serpent with spread hood in each hand.

The language of the grant is Old-Kannada. The grant is dated *Śaka-samvat* 726 (i.e. A.D. 803/4) and records that '. . . when the king [the Rāṣṭrakūṭa *Mahārājādhirāja* Gōyinda (Gōvindarāja III) Prabhūtavarṣa], in the increasing time of his reign, having conquered Dantiga who ruled over Kañchi, had come to levy tribute, and when his encampments were on the bank of the river Tuṅgabhadre, and when, having at his first visit approved of the *tīrtha* called Rāmēśvara, he came there again to spear the boars that had been preserved,—having seen that the *tīrtha* was an excellent one he allotted to the *Gorava* named Śivadhāri . . . the grant of the king Kīrttivarmā to the god Parmēśvara . . .'.

J. F. Fleet, 'Sanskrit and Old-Canarese Inscriptions', in *The Indian Antiquary*, vol. xi, pp. 125–7. *Epigraphia Indica*, vol. vii, App. no. 62 (p. 10). L.D. Barnett calculates the date as 4 April, A.D. 804.

IND. CH. 12

Seven copper plates (22×5·5 cm.) held together by a cut copper ring with an irregularly shaped seal (*c.* 3·5×4 cm.) The seal shows, in high relief, an elephant facing to the proper right. The plates are narrower in the middle and have slightly raised rims. They are severely corroded. The outer side of the first plate bears the inscription: *Vinammaya magan—Dasivimmana magan—Dikesamma*; probably the name (or names) of the person(s) who, at one time, owned the seven plates. Lines 1–48 and lines 62–3 are written in Sanskrit. Lines 49–61 and the lines between 64 and the end of the inscription are in Old-Kannada. The language is rather corrupt and the text lacks continuity. Fleet states that without the assistance of the Merkara and Nāgamaṅgala plates translated by Rice in *The Indian Antiquary*, vol. v, p. 138, he would not have been able to decipher them.

The inscription begins with the usual invocations, followed by a reference to the lineage of the Gaṅga kings. The grantor's name is given as Eṟagaṅga governing the Toṟenāḍu Five-hundred, the Koṅgaḷnāḍu Two-thousand, and the Male Thousand. He is reported to have granted a site, or village, called Panekōḍupādi. No date is given. The grant might be a ninth-century fabrication.

J. F. Fleet, 'Sanskrit and Old-Canarese Inscriptions', in *The Indian Antiquary*, vol. xiv, pp. 229–33. *Epigraphia Indica*, vol. vii, App. no. 116 (p. 21).

IND. CH. 13

Three copper plates (22×8·5 cm.) held together by a cut copper ring with a round seal (2 cm. diameter). The seal shows, in relief on a countersunk surface, a standing elephant facing to the proper left. The third plate is damaged.

The language is Sanskrit until line ten; then a mixture of Sanskrit and Old-Kannada has been used. The grant claims to have been drawn up in *Śaka-samvat* 169 [i.e. A.D. 247/8] and records '. . . a gift of him who is Arivarmā [i.e. the Gaṅga *Mahārājādhirāja* Arivarman (Harivarman)]. When 169 years had expired in the *Śaka* era, in the Prabhava *samvatsara*,—a Bauddha disputant, named Vādimadagajēndra, in the pride of his learning published a paper in the doorway of the palace [of the city] of Taḷavanapura to the effect that he was pre-eminent in logic and grammar and all other kinds of knowledge. And when Mādhavabhaṭṭa, the son of Gōvindabhaṭṭa, of the Bhṛgu *gotra* having declared the meaning of that paper in detail, established the existence of the living soul,—while his opponent maintained the non-existence of the living soul,—and vanquished Vādimadagajēndra with the elephant-goad of his theory,—the king was pleased, and conferred on Mādhavabhaṭṭa the *paṭṭa* of 'a lion to the elephants which are disputants', and, on Friday, the day of the new-moon of *Phālguṇa* under the *Rēvatī-nakṣatra*, and in the Vṛddhi *yoga* and while the sun was in conjunction with the Bull, gave him, free from all opposing claims, and to continue as long as the moon and the sun might last, the village of Oṟekōḍu in the Maisunāḍu Seventy . . .' The grant has often been called a tenth-century forgery but R. Nagaswamy, Director of Archaeology (Madras), who examined the plates during a recent visit to London, believes them to be genuine. The plates were found at Tanjore.

J. F. Fleet, 'Sanskrit and Old-Canarese Inscriptions', in *The Indian Antiquary*, vol. viii, pp. 212–15. A. C. Burnell, *Elements of South Indian Paleography*, revised edition, p. 34. *Epigraphia Indica*, vol. vii, App. no. 108 (p. 20).

IND. CH. 14

Five copper plates (26 × 10 cm.) with raised rims held together by a cut copper ring with a round seal (8 cm. diameter). The legend *Śrī Tribhuvanāṃkuśa* is written across the centre of the seal. Above it are the moon and an elephant-goad, below it a boar facing to the proper left, a *śaṅkha*-shell, two *cauris*, two lamp-stands, and a floral device.

Ind. Ch. 14. Seal

The language of the grant is Sanskrit, the characters are Old-Kannada. After the customary invocations the history of the Eastern Cāḷukyas is discussed until the time of Kulōttunga Cōḍa II in whose reign the grant was made. The grantor is Kolani Kāṭamanāyaka, apparently Governor of the city of Sarasīpurī who, in *Śaka-samvat* 1056 (i.e. A.D. 1134/5), gave the two villages of Maṇḍadoṟṟu and Ponduvagrāma to a number of learned Brahmins.

The plates were found at Chellur.

J. F. Fleet, 'Sanskrit and Old-Canarese Inscriptions', in *The Indian Antiquary*, vol. vii, p. 253, and vol. xiv, pp. 55–9. *Epigraphia Indica*, vol. vii, App. no. 574 (p. 98).

IND. CH. 15

Five copper plates (24·5 × 13 cm.) with raised rims held together by a thick, cut copper ring with a circular seal (8 cm. diameter). The seal has, in relief on a countersunk surface, the legend *Śrī Tribhuvanāṁkuśa* written across the centre. Above it are a boar facing to the proper left, the sun and the moon, two *cauris*, a double drum, a *śaṅkha*-shell, and, close to the moon, something which may be the head of a spear (*kunta*). Below the legend are a floral device, an elephant-goad, a closed lotus on its stalk, and, apparently, a representation of the character *ga*.

The language is Sanskrit, except for a few genitive cases in Kannada. The characters are Old-Kannada, typical of the period to which the grant belongs. The first plate has a raised rim on the outer as well as on the inner side. The inner side shows traces of twelve lines written in an older, more square-looking type of the same alphabet. These lines have been beaten out.

The text begins with a puranic genealogy followed by a narration of historical traditions based on puranic myths about the arrival of the Cāḷukyas in Southern India. This in turn is followed by a list of Eastern Cāḷukya kings until Rājarāja II, also called Viṣṇuvardhana, who ascended the throne in *Śaka-samvat* 944 (i.e. A.D. 1022/3). The grant was made during his reign on the occasion of an eclipse of the moon. It gives the village of Korumelli in the Guddavāḍi *viṣaya* to a Brahmin named Cīḍamārya.

The plates were found at Korumelli.

J. F. Fleet, 'Sanskrit and Old-Canarese Inscriptions', in *The Indian Antiquary*, vol. xiv, pp. 48–55, and vol. vii, p. 253. *Telugu Sasanams*, vol. i, p. 73. *Epigraphia Indica*, vol. vii, App. no. 569 (p. 97).

IND. CH. 16

Seven copper plates (19 × 10 cm.) held together by a cut copper ring with a round seal (7 cm. diameter). The seal bears some kind of inscription.

The language of the grant is Sanskrit. The grant was made by the Vākāṭaka *Mahārāja* Pravarasēna II, the son of Rudrasēna II, at the instance of Koṇḍarāja.

The plates were found at Chammak, East Berar.

J. F. Fleet, *Inscriptions of the Early Gupta Kings*, p. 236. *Epigraphia Indica*, vol. v, App. no. 619 (p. 84).

IND. CH. 17

Two copper plates with raised rims, designed to fit into each other. One plate is 44 × 26 cm., the other is slightly smaller. Ring holes at the bottom of the first and the upper part of the second plate indicate that at one time they were held together by a now lost ring. The language of the grant is Sanskrit, the characters belong to the *Nāgarī* alphabet.

The grant was made by the *Mahārājādhirāja* Gōvindacandra of Kanauj and the *Mahārājaputra* Rājyapāla. It records the gift of land in the Hathauṇḍā *pattalā* to the Ṭhakkur Dēvarāma and his two brothers; but the names which appear on the first plate in line 23 do not seem to be the original ones. Those have apparently been punched out to make room for the present substitutes. The grant was made in *Vikrama-samvat* 1199 (i.e. A.D. 1142).

The plates were found at Gagaha.

L. D. Barnett, 'Gagaha Plates of Govindachandra of Kanauj: Samvat 1199', in *Epigraphia Indica*, vol. xiii, pp. 216–20. F. Kielhorn, 'Copper-plate Grants of the Kings of Kanauj', in *The Indian Antiquary*, vol. xviii, pp. 20–1. *Epigraphia Indica*, vol. v, App. no. 119 (p. 18). A. Carlleyle, *Archaeological Survey of India*, vol. xxii, p. 59.

IND. CH. 18

One copper plate (26·5 × 16 cm. See p. 12).

The language is Hindi. The grant was issued by the *Mahārājādhirāja* Māhādatta Sēna Bahādur. It confers the office of hereditary judge (ḳāẓī) and the possession of a tenth of the lands of Palpā on Raṇa Mardana Sēna. The top of the copper plate is inscribed with the legend *Śri-Bhavāni-Hṛṣikēśau jayataḥ* 1; underneath is written *patra sahī*. Then follows a circle (6·5 cm. diameter) containing the legend *Svasti śrī Sadasiva-caraṇa-man-Māhādata-Sēna-Bahādura-dēvānā* [sic], surrounded by various symbols. Below it, in corrupt Sanskrit, comes the preamble *Svasti Śrīśvara-caraṇa-smaraṇa-pūrvaka-Rūpanārāyanety-ādī-vividha-virudāvali-virājamānmānō bhat śrīman-māhārājadhirāja-śrī-śrī-śrīman-Māhādatta-Sēna-Bāhādura-dēvānāṃ sadā samara-vijaināṃ* [sic]. Then follows the actual grant written in Hindi which is dated *samvat* 1845, *Āṣāḍha kṛṣṇa* 13, *rōz* 7 (A.D. 1789?). The grant was drawn up by Śrīkṛṣṇa Paṇḍita at Pālpāgramma (sic).

IND. CH. 19

Two copper plates (27 × 19 cm.) held together by two rings. One ring is cut, the other ring is furnished with a partly damaged seal. The seal

Ind. Ch. 18

shows, on a sunken surface, the inscription *Śrī Dadda* and a square emblem of undistinguishable character.

The language is Sanskrit. The grant itself is of rather dubious authenticity. It is supposed to have been made by the Gurjara *Mahārājādhirāja* Dadda II Praśāntarāga at Bharukaccha who '. . . presented the village of Tatha-Umbarā [i.e. the modern Bagumra where the plates were found] to a Brāhmaṇa on the occasion of an eclipse of the sun, which happened on the new-moon day of the month *Jyaiṣṭha*, when 415 years of the *Śaka* king had elapsed . . .' (i.e. A.D. 493/4).

The plates were found at Bagumra.

G. Bühler, 'Gurjara Inscriptions, no. iii. A New Grant of Dadda II, or Prasantaraga', in *The Indian Antiquary*, vol. xvii, pp. 183–200. *Epigraphia Indica*, vol. v, App. no. 348 (p. 49).

IND. CH. 20

Two flat copper plates (20 × 14 cm.). Holes through the lower part of the first and the upper part of the second suggest that once they were held together by a ring, now lost. Only the inner side of each plate is inscribed.

The language is Sanskrit, but full of mistakes. The script, typical for the period when the grant was drawn up, is, however, rather badly executed.

The grant records the gift of the village of Balisa in the *āhāra* of Trēyaṇṇā to a Brahmin named Bappasvāmin Dīkṣita. The grantor was the Sēndraka king Pṛthivīvallabha Nikumbhallaśakti. The grant was made in the year 406 of the *Cēdi* era (i.e. A.D. 654/5).

The plates were found at Bagumra.

G. Bühler, 'Bagumra Grant of Nikumbhallasakti; dated in the year 406', in *The Indian Antiquary*, vol. xviii, pp. 265–70. G. Bühler, 'Über eine Sendraka Inschrift aus Gujarāt', in *Sitzungsbericht der Wiener Akademie*, Band cxiv, p. 169. *Epigraphia Indica*, vol. v, App. no. 399 (p. 56).

IND. CH. 21

Five copper plates (20 × 11 cm.) with raised rims held together by a large copper ring with a circular seal (8 cm. diameter). The script is excellently preserved but the seal has suffered severe damage. It seems that at one time the legend *Śrī Tribhuvanāṁkuśa* was written across the centre; above it are representations of the sun, the moon, a boar facing to the proper left, and below it are a floral device and an elephant-goad.

The language is Sanskrit. The grantor is the Eastern Cāḷukya *Mahārājādhirāja* Bhīma II, also called Cāḷukya Bhīma II Viṣṇuvardhana and Gaṇḍa-Mahēndra. The inscription records the grant of the village of Diggubaṟṟu in the *viṣaya* of Pāgunavara to a Brahmin named Viddamayya of the Gautama *gotra*. No specific date is given.

The plates were found at Paganavaram.

J. F. Fleet, 'Sanskrit and Old-Canarese Inscriptions', in *The Indian Antiquary*, vol. xiii, pp. 213–15. *Epigraphia Indica*, vol. vii, App. no. 560 (p. 95).

IND. CH. 22

Three copper plates (19 × 10 cm.) held together by a cut copper ring with a circular seal (7 cm. diameter). The plates have slightly raised rims; one plate is partly damaged. Across the centre of the seal, in relief on a countersunk surface, appears the legend *Śrī Tribhuvanāṁkuśa*. Above it are the sun, the moon, an elephant-goad, two sceptres (or lamp-stands?), and a standing boar facing to the proper left. Underneath the legend are a floral device and a conch-shell.

The language is Sanskrit, except for a few Telugu words. The grant was made by the Eastern Cāḷukya *Mahārājādhirāja* Cāḷukya Bhīma II Viṣṇuvardhana, described as '. . . the son of Mēḻāmbā and Vijayāditya . . .'. At the occasion of the sun's progress to the north, the king granted a field in the village of Ākulamannaṇḍu in the Gudravāta-*viṣaya* to a student of the *kramapāṭha* named Viddammaya. No definite date is given.

The plates seem to have been found at Masulipatam.

F. Kielhorn, 'Masulipatam (?) Plates of Châlukya-Bhîma II' [A.D. 934–945], in *Epigraphia Indica*, vol. v, pp. 132–9. *Epigraphia Indica*, vol. vii, App. no. 561 (p. 95).

IND. CH. 23

Five copper plates (22·5 × 7·5 cm.) held together by a copper ring with a circular seal (6·5 cm. diameter). The ring is not cut but one end is loose in its socket. The plates have raised rims and are partly damaged by corrosion. The legend *Śrī Tribhuvanāṁkuśa* is written across the centre of the seal. Above it are the sun and the moon, underneath is a floral device.

The language is Sanskrit. The grantor was the Eastern Cāḷukya Narēndramṛgarāja Vijayāditya II, who gave the village of Koṟṟapaṟṟu to twenty-four learned Brahmins. No date is given.

J. F. Fleet, 'Sanskrit and Old-Canarese Inscriptions', in *The Indian Antiquary*, vol. xx, pp. 414–18. E. Hultzsch, *South Indian Inscriptions*, vol. i, p. 31. *Epigraphia Indica*, vol. vii, App. no. 553 (p. 93).

IND. CH. 24

Five copper plates (21 × 11 cm.) with raised rims held together by a cut copper ring with a round seal (8 cm. diameter). The upper part of the seal shows, in relief on a countersunk surface, the sun, the moon, and an elephant-goad; below it is written the legend *Śrī Tribhuvan*[*ā*]*ṁ-ku*[*śa*]*ḥ*. The centre of the seal is occupied by a standing boar, and in the lowest part of the seal is a half-open lotus.

The language is mainly Sanskrit mixed with some occasional Telugu passages. The script belongs to the southern class of the alphabet and the individual letters have not been cut very deeply.

The grant was made by the Eastern Cāḷukya *Mahārājādhirāja* Ammarāja II (Vijayāditya VI), who ruled between A.D. 945 and 970. The text records the gift of the village of Kaluchumbaṟṟu to a Jain teacher named Arhanandin, made for the purpose of repairing the charitable dining-hall of the Jain temple Sarvalōkāśraya Jinabhavana. The king made the grant at the request of a certain lady called Chāme-kāmbā, apparently a professional courtesan and one of the king's mistresses. No definite date is given.

J. F. Fleet, 'Kaluchumbarru Grant of Amma II', in *Epigraphia Indica*, vol. vii, pp. 177–92. *Epigraphia Indica*, vol. vii, App. no. 1065 (p. 166).

IND. CH. 25

Five copper plates (26 × 15 cm.) with raised rims held together by a large, cut copper ring with a round seal (7 cm. diameter). The legend *Śrī Tribhuvan*[*āṁ*]*kuśa* is written across the centre of the seal. Above it, in relief on a countersunk surface, a standing boar facing to the proper left is surrounded by the sun, the moon, an elephant-goad, two *cauris*, two lamp-stands, and a conch-shell. Underneath the legend is a lotus, a drum, a swastika, and a device which may be the character *ga*, or the representation of a throne.

The language is Sanskrit written in Old-Kannada characters. The script is well preserved except for lines 103–9 which show traces of intentional interference.

The grant was made by the *Mahārājādhirāja* Vīracōḍadēva, otherwise called Viṣṇuvardhana, of the Eastern Cāḷukya family who ruled over the

Vēṅgī country. It is a Vaiṣṇava inscription recording the gift of the village of Koleṟu to a temple of Viṣṇu in Chellur. The genealogical part is exceptionally long and discusses the puranic, mythological, and historical origins of the Western and Eastern Cāḷukyas at great length. Vīracōḍadēva became viceroy of Vēṅgī around A.D. 1078. The grant is supposed to have been made in the twenty-first year of his reign.

The plates were found at Chellur.

J. F. Fleet, 'Chellur Copper-plate Grant of Vira-Chodadeva', in *The Indian Antiquary*, vol. xix, pp. 423–36. E. Hultzsch, *South Indian Inscriptions*, vol. i, p. 49. *Epigraphia Indica*, vol. vii, App. no. 572 (p. 98).

IND. CH. 26

Eight copper plates (25 × 14 cm.) held together by a large, cut copper ring without seal.

The language is Sanskrit except for some Telugu passages. It is written in Telugu characters typical of the period in question. The grant was made by the *Mahārāja* Allaya Vēma Reḍḍi in Rajahmundry and records how the village of Vēmavaram was 'joyfully bestowed' on a number of 'excellent Brahmins'. The names of the donees, their places of origin, fathers' names, and *gotras* are given in great detail in verses 32–112. The grant is dated *Śaka-samvat* 1356 (i.e. A.D. 1434).

The plates were found at Rajahmundry.

L. D. Barnett, 'Vemavaram Grant of Allaya-Vema Reddi: Saka 1356', in *Epigraphia Indica*, vol. xiii, pp. 237–59.

IND. CH. 27

Three copper plates (27 × 11 cm.) held together by a cut copper ring. In place of the customary seal a kneeling bull has been soldered on to the ring.

The grant is written in a mixture of Sanskrit and Telugu. The text opens with nineteen Sanskrit verses followed by the names of the twenty donees in Sanskrit prose. Then the boundaries of the granted village are discussed in Telugu prose. After this come five verses in Sanskrit and a concluding Telugu sentence.

The grant records how '. . . in the *Śaka* year . . . 1296 [i.e. A.D. 1374/5] . . . the king Aṇṇa-Vēma [of Koṇḍavīṭu] gave to *Brāhmaṇs* the excellent village called Naḍupūru in Kōṇasthala, for the religious merit of his sister, the illustrious Vēmasāni . . .'.

E. Hultsch, 'Nadupuru Grant of Anna-Vema; Saka-Samvat 1296', in *Epigraphia Indica*, vol. iii, pp. 286–92. *Epigraphia Indica*, vol. vii, App. no. 593 (p. 103).

IND. CH. 28

Three copper plates (20·5 × 8 cm.) held together by a cut copper ring with a circular seal (5 cm. diameter). The middle of the seal shows

Ind. Ch. 28

in relief the Pallava emblem: a humped bull sitting with his right leg stretched in front of him. On each side of the bull are a lamp-stand, above him five emblems of undistinguishable nature, and below him is a snake-like line. An inscription, running around the outer edge of the seal, is no longer legible.

The language of the grant consists of three Sanskrit verses, a passage in Tamil prose, and a fourth Sanskrit verse at the end. The Sanskrit part is written in *Grantha*; the Tamil part in Tamil characters with an occasional word written in *Grantha*. The Sanskrit portion deals with the usual invocations and with genealogical references. The Tamil section contains the actual grant made in the fourteenth regnal year of the Pallava king Vijaya Skandaśiṣya Vikramavarman (i.e. during the eighth century A.D.) at the request of his feudatory Mahāvali Vāṇarāya. The grant informs the inhabitants of the district of Paḍuvūr-kōṭṭam and the inhabitants of Mēl Aḍiayāṟu-nāḍu, a sub-division of the same district, that the village of Śārugūr has been given to a Brahmin.

The plates were found at Rayakota in the Salem district.

E. Hultzsch, 'Rayakota Plates of Skandasishya', in *Epigraphia Indica*, vol. v, pp. 49–53. *Epigraphia Indica*, vol. vii, App. no. 644 (p. 110).

IND. CH. 29

Five copper plates (24×17 cm.) with rounded tops held together by a cut copper ring with a circular seal (4 cm. diameter), which is movable. It is decorated with the raised figure of a boar and some other emblems.

The language is Sanskrit with a sprinkling of Tamil words. The plates refer to the reign of Veṅkaṭapati I of Karṇāṭa and his ancestors. They are dated *Śaka-samvat* 1535 (i.e. A.D. 1613) and record the grant of the village of Kāṭrapāḍi Cinnatimmapuram in the province of Paḍavīḍu to a number of Brahmins.

L. D. Barnett, 'Two Grants of Venkatapati: Saka 1508 and 1535', in *Epigraphia Indica*, vol. xiii, pp. 231–7.

IND. CH. 30

Five copper plates with rounded tops (18/23×1·7 cm.) held together by a cut copper ring with circular seal (3 cm. diameter). The seal, made movable by an additional ring, is decorated with the representation of a boar.

The language of the grant is Sanskrit, the script *Nandināgarī*. The grant was issued by the *Mahārāja* Raṅgarāya II of Karṇāṭa in *Śaka-samvat* 1566 (i.e. A.D. 1644/5). The kings of Karṇāṭa were the successors of the kings of Vijayanagar. The grant records the gift of the village of Kaḷḷakurśi, situated in the kingdom of Tiruvadi, to a Brahmin named Koṇḍappa. The composition of the stanzas is ascribed to Rāma, the son of Kāmakoṭi. The engraver's name was Somanāthārya, son of Kāmaya.

The plates seem to have been found at Chingleput.

E. Hultzsch, 'Karṇâṭa Grants no. ii. A Grant of Raṅga II, dated 1644–5 A.D.', in *The Indian Antiquary*, vol. xiii, p. 153. *Epigraphia Indica*, vol. vii, App. no. 545 (p. 92).

IND. CH. 31

Five copper plates with arched tops (18/24 × 17 cm.) held together by a cut copper ring with circular seal (4 cm. diameter), which is movable. It shows, in relief, a boar standing on a kind of platform, the sun, the moon, and what appears to be an elephant-goad.

The language of the grant is Sanskrit, the script *Nandināgarī*. The plates are numbered by Kannada characters.

The grant refers to the reign of the *Mahārāja* Veṅkaṭapati I of Karṇāṭa who gave the villages of Yampēḍu and Battulapalli to a Brahmin named Kalimili Kṛṣṇabhaṭṭa. The poet who composed the stanzas was Kṛṣṇa, the engraver's name was Gaṇapayācārya. The grant is dated *Śaka-samvat* 1508 (i.e. A.D. 1586).

The plates were found at Chittur.

L. D. Barnett, 'Two Grants of Venkatapati I. Saka 1508 and 1535', in *Epigraphia Indica*, vol. xiii, pp. 225–31.

IND. CH. 32

Seven copper plates with arched tops (20/25 × 18 cm.) held together by a cut copper ring with round seal (4 cm. diameter). The seal shows a boar, the sun, and the moon. The plates have raised rims for the protection of the script.

The language of the grant is Sanskrit, the script *Nandināgarī*. The plates are numbered by Kannada characters and the last word of the grant is written in large Kannada letters.

The plates record the grant of thirty villages by Sadāśiva Rāya, king of Vijayanagar, to members of the Rāmānuja sect living near the birth-place of the late Vaiṣṇava saint. The boundaries of the villages are described in great detail. The grant was made in *Śaka-samvat* 1478 (i.e. A.D. 1556).

The plates were found at Chingleput.

F. Kielhorn, 'British Museum plates of Sadasivaraya, Saka-samvat 1478', in *Epigraphia Indica*, vol. iv, pp. 1–22. *Epigraphia Indica*, vol. vii, App. no. 530 (p. 89).

IND. CH. 33

One copper plate (29×16 cm.), broken in two. The upper part of the plate shows an engraved ornamental circle, a legend, and various floral devices.

The language of the grant is Hindi, the script *Devanāgarī*. The inscription records a land-grant made by the *Mahārāja* Mukunda Sēna Bahādur, of the same state and period and in the same style as *Ind. Ch. 18* above. The grant is dated *Samvat* 1836, *Faṣlī* 1187, *Phālguna śu.* 7; which L. D. Barnett translated into 13 March, A.D. 1780.

IND. CH. 34

One copper plate (33×25 cm. See p. 21). Small strips of copper are fastened by rivets along the edges of the plate to protect the script and a copper ring is attached to the top.

The language of the grant is Sanskrit written by somebody who was either careless or ignorant. The script is *Devanāgrī* of the twelfth century A.D. The grant records the gift of the village of Ahaḍāpāḍa in the Khaṇḍagahā *pattalā* to two Brahmins: the Ṭhakur Mahāditya and the Ṭhakur Śīlaṇa, both sons of the Ṭhakur Caturbhuja. The grantor was the *Mahārāṇaka* Kīrttivarman of Kakkarēḍikā, apparently a feudatory of the Cēdi ruler Jayasimhadēva. The grant is dated in the *Cēdi* year 926 (i.e. A.D. 1174/5).

F. Kielhorn, 'Four Rewah Copper-plate Inscriptions', in *The Indian Antiquary*, vol. xvii, pp. 224–7. The Rewah plates (Ind. Ch. 34—Ind. Ch. 37) were first described by Sir A. Cunningham in the *Archaeological Survey of India*, vol. xxi, pp. 145–8. F. Kielhorn edited them at J. F. Fleet's request in *The Indian Antiquary*, vol. xvii, pp. 227–35. At the end of his article Kielhorn gives a genealogy of the *Mahārāṇakas* of Kakkarēḍikā, as deduced from the inscriptions. *Epigraphia Indica*, vol. v, App. no. 419 (p. 60).

IND. CH. 35

One flat copper plate (39×23 cm.), badly corroded.

The language is a very faulty Sanskrit, the script *Devanāgarī*. The grant informs the people that the *Mahārāṇaka* Salakhaṇavarmadēva Kakkarēḍikā, who evidently owed allegiance to the Cēdi ruler Vijayadēva, gave the village of Chiḍauḍā, in the Kūyīsavapālisa *pattalā*, to a number of Brahmins, all great-grandsons of the Ṭhakur Mādhava. The date is given as *Vikrama-samvat* 1253 (i.e. A.D. 1195).

F. Kielhorn, 'Four Rewah Copper-plate Inscriptions', in *The Indian Antiquary*, vol. xvii, pp. 227–30. *Epigraphia Indica*, vol. v, App. no. 186 (p. 27).

Ind. Ch. 34

IND. CH. 36

Two copper plates, one (30×23 cm.) flat, the other (32×24 cm.) with raised rims (see p. 22). The plates are designed to fit into each other. The script is on the inside of the plates except for the names of the six donees which appear additionally on the outside of the first plate.

The language is Sanskrit, the script *Devanāgarī*. The grant was made by the *Mahārāṇaka* Kumārapāladēva of Kakkarēḍikā; like most of his ancestors a devout Śaivite.

Ind. Ch. 36

The plates record the gift of the village of Rēhī to the six sons of *Rāuta* Aṇavapāla. The names of the donees are Sāṅgē, Sūhaḍa, Mahāita, Ramasiha, Sōmīvījhū, and Sāvantaśaraman. The grant is dated *Vikrama-samvat* 1297 (i.e. A.D. 1239).

F. Kielhorn, 'Four Rewah Copper-plate Inscriptions', in *The Indian Antiquary*, vol. xvii, pp. 230–4. *Epigraphia Indica*, vol. v, App. no. 218 (p. 32).

IND. CH. 37

Two copper plates (29×19 cm. and 28×18 cm. respectively). The larger plate is inscribed on one side only, the smaller plate bears inscriptions on both sides; they are designed to fit into each other. The larger plate has raised rims, the smaller plate is flat but protected by copper bands fixed with rivets round the edges. Holes in the lower part of the first and the upper part of the second plate indicate that at one time they were held together by a ring, now lost.

The language of the grant is Sanskrit, the script *Devanāgarī*. Writer and engraver seem to have been rather careless.

This is the last of the four Rewah plates edited by F. Kielhorn in vol. xvii of *The Indian Antiquary*. The text of the grant follows the usual pattern: invocations, references to the lineage of the Kakkarēḍikā rulers, followed by the actual grant. The grantor's name is *Mahārāṇaka* Harirājadēva. He informs the people that he has given the village of Agasēyi in the Vadharā *pattalā* to the *Rāutas* Sāngē, Sūhaḍa, Mahāditya, and Sāmanatha, the sons of the *Rāuta* Aṇavē, and to a man named Rāmasimha whose lineage is duly given. The boundaries of the various estates are well described. The grant is dated *Vikrama-samvat* 1298 (i.e. A.D. 1240).

F. Kielhorn, 'Four Rewah Copper-plate Inscriptions', in *The Indian Antiquary*, vol. xvii, pp. 234–5. *Epigraphia Indica*, vol. v, App. no. 219 (p. 32).

IND. CH. 38

One flat copper plate (25×18 cm.), inscribed on one side only.

The language of the grant is Hindi, the script *Devanāgarī*. The text records how the *Mahārāja* Rāvēndra Ṣāḥib Balabhadra Siṃha conveyed the villages of Vīradatta (Bīrdatt) and Majhigawā, in the Kharam Sēṛā *parganā*, to the Princess (*Mahārājakumārī*) Lālā Padum Kuvari. The grantor was a brother of the *Mahārāja* Viśvanātha Siṃha and held the *parganā* of Amar Patan for his maintenance. The grant was written by Gajarāja on *Jesṭh sudi* 5 of *Samvat* 1892 (A.D. 1836?).

IND. CH. 39

One flat copper plate (23×11 cm.), inscribed on one side only (see p. 25).

The language of the grant is Hindi, the script *Devanāgarī*. The text records how the *Mahārājakumāra Bābū* Balabharda Siṃha, the son of Jai Siṅgh, conveyed the village of Karhīl in the *parganā* of Kharam Sēṛā for the cult of Rāma in the temple of Akṣayavaṭa at Citrakūṭa (in the Banda District, U.P.). The priest in charge of the temple was Lāldāsjī. The grant was written by Lālā Dāmodaraprasāda, and is dated *Āśvina sudi* 10 of *Samvat* 1883 (A.D. 1827?).

IND. CH. 40

One flat copper plate (21×13 cm.), inscribed on one side only.

The language of the grant is Hindi, the script *Devanāgarī*. The grant was made by the same Balabhadra Siṃha as the previous grant. It assigns the village of Cakērā in the *parganā* of Kharam Sēṛā to a man named Kolai Rām. The grant was written on *Asāṛh badi* 1 of *Samvat* 1885 (A.D. 1829?), at the office of Lālā Gajarāja.

IND. CH. 41

One flat copper plate (18×15 cm.), inscribed on one side only.

The language of the grant is Hindi, the script *Devanāgarī*. It is a notification from Rāvēndra Balabhadra Siṃha, announcing to the residents of Majhigawā and Bīrdatt that he has assigned these villages to the Princess Padum Kuvari (see *Ind. Ch. 38*). The grant is dated *Jeṣṭha śudi 5*, *Samvat* 1892 (A.D. 1836?).

IND. CH. 42

Three copper plates (27×18·5 cm.) with raised rims, held together by a cut copper ring with a circular seal (7 cm. diameter). The seal shows, in very high relief on a slightly countersunk surface, the sun, the moon, and a dancing figure which Fleet describes as Hanumān (see p. 26).

The language is Sanskrit, the script *Nandināgarī*. The grant was made under the reign of the Dēvagiri Yādava king Kanhara (Kṛṣṇa), the son of Jaitugi II. It records that in the Saumya *samvatsara*, when *Śaka* 1171 (i.e. A.D. 1249/50) had expired, the minister Mallisaiṭṭi, with the king's permission, bestowed upon thirty-two Brahmins attached to the shrine of the god Mādhava, certain lands at Santheya Bāgavāḍi in the Huvvalli

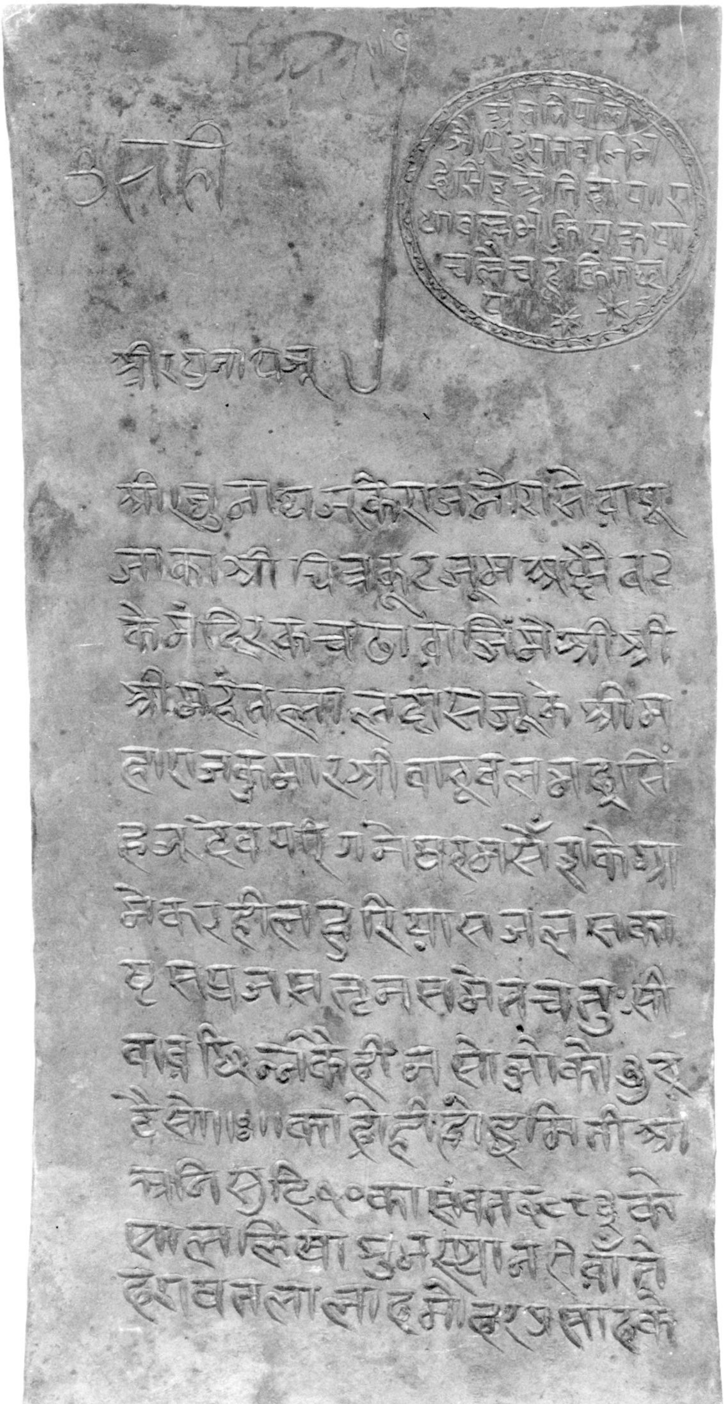

Ind. Ch. 39

Twelve in the Kuhuṇḍi district. The grant was subsequently confirmed by Mallisaiṭṭi's son, the minister Cauṇḍisaiṭṭi.

The plates were found at Chikka Bagewadi.

J. F. Fleet, 'Sanskrit and Old-Canarese Inscriptions', in *The Indian Antiquary*, vol. vii, pp. 303–8. *Epigraphia Indica*, vol. vii, App. no. 357 (p. 64).

Ind. Ch. 42. Seal

IND. CH. 43

One copper plate (31 × 22 cm.), badly damaged at the corners. It is the second and last plate of a grant, the first plate seems to have been lost.

The language is Sanskrit. The grantor was the *Mahārāja* Guhasēna of Valabhī; the grant itself was written by Skandabhaṭa, Minister of Peace and War. It records the gift of four villages to '. . . the reverend Śākya monks, belonging to the eighteen schools [of the *Hīnayāna*] who have come from various directions to the great convent of Duḍḍā, built by the venerable Duḍḍā . . .', a sister's daughter of Dhruvasēna, another Valabhī king. Bühler reads the date as '. . . 266 in the dark half of *Māghā* . . .' of the *Gupta-Valabhī* era (i.e. A.D. 585), while Kielhorn thinks the grant was made in the year 246 of the *Valabhī* era (i.e. A.D. 565).

The plates were found at Wala.

J. G. Bühler, 'A grant of King Guhasena of Valabhī', in *The Indian Antiquary*, vol. iv, p. 174. F. Kielhorn, 'A List of Inscriptions of Northern India about

A.D. 400', in *Epigraphia Indica*, vol. v, pp. 1–96. *Epigraphia Indica*, vol. xiii, p. 338 (see an article by L. D. Barnett), and vol. v, App. no. 465 (p. 66).

IND. CH. 44

One copper plate (47×31 cm.) with a ring hole at the top. The ring hole consists of a copper band held by rivets. The bell-shaped seal is exceptionally large and heavy. It shows, in relief, the goddess Lakṣmī sitting cross-legged in the middle of the seal. She is attended by two elephants who pour water over her. Underneath the goddess is written

Ind. Ch. 44. Seal

Śrimat Karṇadēva, and below this is the representation of a sitting bull with a drum on each side.

The language is Sanskrit. The plate is the first one of a set, the rest have been lost. It is the beginning of a grant made by the Kalacuri King Karṇadēva (Lakṣmī-Karṇa), the son of Gāṅgēya of Cēdi, and contains about twenty verses in praise of his lineage.

E. Hultzsch, 'Goharwa Plates of Karnadeva', in *Epigraphia Indica*, vol. xi, p. 139. The verses praising the king's lineage are the same as the verses at the beginning of the Goharwa Plates Hultzsch discusses in this article. The seals too are almost identical, the difference lies only in the workmanship. The British Museum seal is of much better quality. Hultzsch gives the date A.D. 1047 for the Goharwa plates.

IND. CH. 45

One copper plate (22 × 16 cm.), inscribed on one side only. There are two small holes at the top of the plate.

The language is a mixed dialect, half Hindi and half Gujarati; the script is *Devanāgarī*. The grantor was the *Mahārāja Dīwān* Ajao Singh who gave the village of Salāvad in the *parganā* of Candlāi to Kundan Dāi, the son of Gajapati Dāi.

IND. CH. 46

One copper plate (20 × 18 cm.) with an oval seal (9 × 7 cm.) soldered into the left side.

The language is Sanskrit. The grant is of dubious authenticity. It is supposed to have been made by Samudragupta, in the Gupta year 9 (*c.* fifth century A.D.) at Ayōdhyā.

The plates were found at Gaya.

J. F. Fleet, *Inscriptions of the Early Gupta Kings*, p. 254. *Epigraphia Indica*, vol. v, App. no. 511 (p. 71).

IND. CH. 47

Two copper plates (26 × 17 cm.) with two holes and a thin ring still attached to one of the plates. The plates are inscribed on one side only. They are badly affected by corrosion, some corners are missing, and the script itself is hardly legible.

The language is Sanskrit. The grant was made by the *Mahārāja* Dhruvasēna of Valabhī in the Gupta year 217 (i.e. A.D. 637).

T. Bloch, *Journal of the Royal Asiatic Society*, 1895, p. 379. *Epigraphia Indica*, vol. v, App. no. 461 (p. 65).

IND. CH. 48

One copper plate (45 × 33 cm.) broken in two. The edges are badly damaged. A hole at the top indicates that once there might have been a ring and a seal.

The language is Sanskrit. The grant was made by Gōvindacandra, *Gāhaḍavāla Mahārāja* of Kanauj. It conveys the village of Jara to a Brahmin named Bhūpati Śarman. The grant is dated *Samvat* 1185 (A.D. 1129?).

The plates were found at Benares.

A. Führer, *Journal of the Asiatic Society of Bengal*, vol. lvi (1887), part 1, p. 118. *Epigraphia Indica*, vol. v, App. no. 100 (p. 16).

IND. CH. 49

One copper plate (37×29 cm.) with a ring hole at the top. The right-hand bottom corner is missing. In some places attempts seem to have been made to beat out the inscription.

The language is Sanskrit. This grant too was made by Gōvindacandra of Kanauj. It conveys the village of Tribhāṇḍī to Bhūpati Śarman. The grant is dated *Samvat* 1181 (A.D. 1125?).

A. Führer, *Journal of the Asiatic Society of Bengal*, vol. lvi (1887), part i, p. 113. *Epigraphia Indica*, vol. v, App. no. 96 (p. 15).

IND. CH. 50

One copper plate (38×27 cm.).

The language is a mixed dialect, half Hindi, half Gujarati. The script is *Devanāgarī*. The grant was made by the *Mahārāu Rājā* Pratāpa Siṃha. It assigns a village to the Brahmins of Jaitpur for the maintenance of the Kṛṣṇa cult. The plate is dated *Vaiśakha badi* 11 in *Samvat* 1845 (A.D. 1789?).

IND. CH. 51

One copper plate (17×13 cm.), inscribed on both sides. A crudely drawn figure of an arrow is incised on the top of the obverse.

The language seems to be a Rajasthani dialect. The script is rather badly executed. The grant was issued by the *Mahārāja* Divānajī Acalasiṃghajī and refers to a hundred *bighās* of land, etc., granted to a Brahmin named Raṇacchōra. The plate is dated *Āśvina badi* 5 of *Samvat* 1843 (A.D. 1787?).

IND. CH. 52

Three copper plates (20×11 cm.) held together by a copper ring with a circular seal (6 cm. diameter). The seal has a string of bead-like ornaments along the edge and shows, in high-relief, a representation of Garuḍa: a device on the banner of the Śilāhāras. Garuḍa is represented as a man with a bird's beak, sitting cross-legged, his hands folded. Wings project from his shoulders; he wears a pointed head-dress and has a halo behind him.

The language is Sanskrit, the characters are ancient *Devanāgarī*. The grant refers to the Śilāhāra *Mahāmaṇḍalēśvara* Chittarāja Dēva, a member of the Śilāhāra family of northern Konkan who gave '. . . to the great Brahmin Āmadevaiya . . . who is devoted to the six duties of sacrifice . . . the field known as the field of Vōḍaṇibhaṭṭa in the village Nōura which lies in the Ṣaṭṣaṣṭī district which is included [in the territory of] the famous Sthānaka . . .'. The grant is dated *Śaka-samvat* 948 (i.e. A.D. 1026).

The plates were found at Bhandup.

J. F. Fleet, 'Bhandup Plates of Chittarajadeva; A.D. 1026', in *Epigraphia Indica*, vol. xii, pp. 250–68. F. Kielhorn, *List of the Inscriptions of Southern India*, vol. vii, App. no. 307. *Epigraphia Indica*, vol. vii, App. no. 307 (p. 55). W. H. Wathen, *Journal of the Royal Asiatic Society*, vol. ii (1835), p. 383. G. Bühler, *The Indian Antiquary*, vol. v (1876), pp. 276–81.

Ind. Ch. 52. Seal

IND. CH. 53

Three copper plates (28 × 19·5 cm.) with slightly raised rims held together by two rings. The left ring is plain and cut; the right ring is uncut, of irregular shape furnished with a circular seal (3 cm. diameter). In the centre of the seal, in relief on a countersunk surface, the god Śiva is represented in a way similar to the seal of *Ind. Ch. 11*.

The language of the grant is Sanskrit. The introductory part discusses certain aspects of the history of the Rāṣṭrakūṭa kings. The grant is dated *Śaka-samvat* 734 (i.e. A.D. 812/13) and records the gift of the village of Vaḍapadraka, in the Ankoṭṭaka 84 circle of villages, to a Brahmin named Bhānu (or Bhānubhaṭṭa) of the Vātsyāyana *gotra*, belonging to the *Caturvēdīs* of Valabhī. Lines 70–4 record that a former king had given that same village to the *Caturvēdīs* of *Anakoṭṭa* but that it had been taken away by another (obviously) evil king. Now Karka II wished to give it to some excellent Brahmin as a reward for his learning. The grantor was the Rāṣṭrakūṭa *Mahāsamantādhipati* Karkarāja Suvarṇavarśa of Gujarat. The fact that he does not use any royal titles may indicate that he was a vassal of a Rāṣṭrakūṭa king of the main line.

The plates were found at Baroda.

J. F. Fleet, 'Sanskrit and Old-Canarese Inscriptions', in *The Indian Antiquary*, vol. xii, pp. 156–65. H. T. Prinsep, *Journal of the Bengal Asiatic Society*, vol. viii, p. 292. *Epigraphia Indica*, vol. vii, App. no. 65 (p. 11).

IND. CH. 54

Five copper plates (21 × 12 cm.) with raised rims held together by a copper ring with oval (4 × 3 cm.) seal showing, on a countersunk surface, a standing boar facing to the proper right.

The language is Sanskrit. The grant gives the genealogy of the Western Cāḷukya king Pulakēsin I Satyāśraya. It mentions one of his feudatories named Sāmiyāra, of the Rundaranīḷa Saindraka family, who was governor of the Kuhuṇḍi district. Sāmiyāra built a Jain temple in the city of Alaktakanagara, the main town in a circle of 700 villages, and, with the king's permission, made certain grants of lands and villages to the temple on the occasion of an eclipse of the moon on the day of the full-moon of the month *Vaiśākha* in the Vibhava *samvatsara* when the *Śaka* year 411 (i.e. A.D. 489/90) had expired.

The plates were found at Altem.

J. F. Fleet, 'Sanskrit and Old-Canarese Inscriptions', in *The Indian Antiquary*, vol. vii, pp. 209–17. (Fleet believes the plates to be a tenth-century forgery.) W. H. Wathen, *Journal of the Royal Asiatic Society*, vol. v, p. 343. *Epigraphia Indica*, vol. vii, App. no. 2 (p. 2).

IND. CH. 55

One copper plate (29/24 × 19 cm.). The top is cut in ornamental curves to a finial.

The language is Tamil. The plate is dated *Kali* 4552 and *Śārvari*, in the reign of Veṅkaṭapati, and records a sale of lands in Karur Taluk, Coimbatore District, to a number of persons by Śinna Kollan Piḷḷai. L. D. Barnett does not accept the authenticity of the plates. *Kali* 4552 current (A.D. 1450/1) corresponded to *Pramoda*. The nearest *Śārvari* (current) was A.D. 1420/1 and 1480/1.

IND. CH. 56

Three copper plates (21 × 14 cm.) held together by a copper ring with a square seal (3·5 × 3 cm.), of which the bottom left corner is missing. The seal has a very high rim and shows, in relief, the sun, the moon, and underneath a boar facing to the proper left.

The language is a rather barbarous Sanskrit written in *Nāgarī* script. The grant is definitely a quite late forgery. It is supposed to have been issued by the Cāḷukya *Mahārājādhirāja* Satyāśraya.

IND. CH. 57

Two copper plates (45 × 12 cm.). The plates (referred to as Plate A and Plate B) are physically independent of each other.

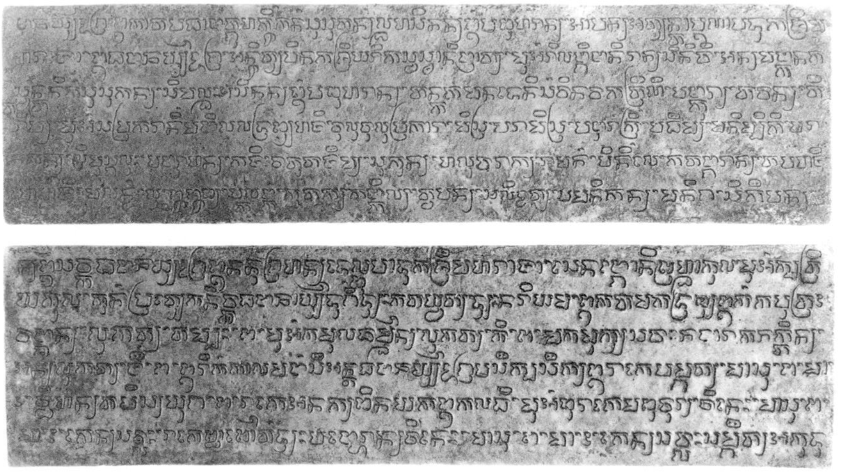

Ind. Ch. 57. Javanese grant

The language of the grant is Javanese. Plate A records the making of a canal in the *lĕmah asinan* of Pabuharan by a teacher named Ugra, with some rights and regulations to be maintained for it. Plate B records a grant of the attributes of the Brahman-order and Kṣatriya-order by the King to Ugra's children named Dyah Kataywat and Dyah Nari-yama, etc.

Dr. Krom, *Verhandelingen b. Bataviaasch Genootschap*, vol. lx (1913), p. 250. Cohen Stuart, *Kawi-Oorkonden*, no. xxx, 2, 3, and 6 (p. 38); xxii, 3 a–b, 1–3 (p. 32); ii, 3b. 4 (p. 7); vii, 4b. 1 (p. 17).

IND. CH. 58

Three copper plates (17×4 cm.) held together by a cut copper ring with square (3×2 cm.) seal showing, according to Fleet, a dog on a countersunk surface.

The seven grants described as *Ind. Ch. 58–Ind. Ch. 64* were found in 1855 by J. F. Fleet in a mound of earth close to a small well called Chakratīrtha, a short distance outside Halsi. They are written in Sanskrit in the so-called cave-alphabet which had not yet developed into proper Old-Kannada characters. All plates record grants made in the fifth century A.D. by an old dynasty of Kadamba kings. The Kadambas were Jains. Each inscription begins on the inside of the first plate, and ends on the inside of the last. The individual plates are held together by thin rings furnished (in most cases) with exceptionally heavy seals. The texts begin usually with 'Reverence! Victorious is the holy one, Jinēndra, who abounds in good qualities, and who is renowned as being extremely compassionate; the banner of his tenderness, which comforts the three words, is lifted up on high . . .'.

Ind. Ch. 58 is the earliest and smallest of the whole set. It also seems to have suffered more damage than most. The grantor was the Kadamba *Yuvarāja* Kākusthavarman who gave a field at the village of Khēṭagrāma to the General Śrutakīrtti.

J. F. Fleet, 'Sanskrit and Old-Canarese Inscriptions', in *The Indian Antiquary*, vol. vi, pp. 23–4. *Journal of the Bombay Branch of the Royal Asiatic Society*, vol. ix, no. xxvii. p. 229. *Epigraphia Indica*, vol. vii, App. no. 602 (p. 105).

IND. CH. 59

Three copper plates (20×7 cm.) held together by a large, thin copper ring with an oval seal (2·5×4 cm.) inscribed with the name *Śrī Mṛgēśvaraḥ* (see p. 34).

The grant records how, in the eighth year of his reign, the Kadamba king Mṛgēśavarman had a Jain temple built at Palāśikā. The king then endowed the temple with a gift of land.

J. F. Fleet, 'Sanskrit and Old-Canarese Inscriptions', in *The Indian Antiquary*, vol. vi, pp. 24–5. *Journal of the Bombay Branch of the Royal Asiatic Society*, vol. ix, no. xxvii, p. 229. *Epigraphia Indica*, vol. vii, App. no. 606 (p. 105).

IND. CH. 60

Five copper plates (19×6 cm.) held together by a thin copper ring with a bulky, square seal (3×2 cm.). The device on the seal has almost entirely disappeared but there is a certain similarity to the 'dog' on *Ind. Ch. 58*.

The grant was made by the Kadamba king Ravivarmā who gave the village of Purukhēṭaka to the mother of his own father. '. . . the Lord Ravi established the ordinance at the mighty city of Palāśikā, that the

Ind. Ch. 59

glory of Jinēndra, [the festival of which] lasts eight days, should be celebrated every year on the full moon of *Kārttika* from the revenues of that village; that ascetics should be supported during the four months of the rainy season, that learned men, the chief of whom was Kumāradatta . . . should according to justice enjoy all the material substances of that greatness; and that the worship of Jinēndra should be perpetually performed by the pious countrymen and citizens . . .'

J. F. Fleet, 'Sanskrit and Old-Canarese Inscriptions', in *The Indian Antiquary*, vol. vi, pp. 25–7. *Journal of the Bombay Branch of the Royal Asiatic Society*, vol. ix, no. xxvii, p. 229. *Epigraphia Indica*, vol. vii, App. no. 608 (p. 106).

IND. CH. 61

Three copper plates (15×5 cm.) held together by a thin ring with an oval seal (2·5×3·5 cm.). The characters on the seal are no longer legible. The inscription records how '. . . land of the measure of fifteen *nivartanas*, in the field called Kardamapaṭī at Palāśikā, free from the gleaning-tax and all other burdens was assigned in a copper charter [and so was given] on the tenth lunar day of the sixth fortnight of the winter season in the eleventh year of the reign of the pious Great King Śrī Ravivarmā, by the Bhōjaka Paṇḍara, the worshipper of the supreme *Arhat*, who had acquired the favour of the feet of the glorious kiṅg Bhānuvarmā . . .'.

J. F. Fleet, 'Sanskrit and Old-Canarese Inscriptions', in *The Indian Antiquary*, vol. vi, pp. 27–9. *Journal of the Bombay Branch of the Royal Asiatic Society*, vol. ix, no. xxvii, p. 229. *Epigraphia Indica*, vol. vii, App. no. 610 (p. 106).

IND. CH. 62

Three copper plates (15×5 cm.) held together by a thin ring with a bulky, square seal (3×2 cm.) The device on the badly defaced seal shows a vague resemblance to the 'dog' already mentioned. The text records a grant made by the Kadamba king Ravivarmā who gave 'four *nivartanas* of land' to another Jain establishment.

J. F. Fleet, 'Sanskrit and Old-Canarese Inscriptions', in *The Indian Antiquary*, vol. vi, pp. 29–30. *Journal of the Bombay Branch of the Royal Asiatic Society*, vol. ix, no. xxvii, p. 229. *Epigraphia Indica*, vol. vii, App. no. 609 (p. 106).

IND. CH. 63

Three copper plates (16×15 cm.) held together by a thin small ring with a bulky oval seal (4×3 cm.). The seal is inscribed with the name *Śrī Harivarmā*. The grant records how the Kadamba king Harivarmā, in his fourth regnal year, gave the village of Vasuntavāṭaka in the district of Suddikundūra to a Jain establishment '. . . for the purpose of providing annually, at the great eight-day sacrifice, the perpetual anointing with clarified butter for the temple of the *Arhat* which Mṛgēśa, the son of the General Siṅha of the lineage of *Bhāradvāja*, had caused to be built at Palāśikā, and that whatever might remain over after this was to be devoted to the purpose of feeding the whole sect . . .'.

J. F. Fleet, 'Sanskrit and Old-Canarese Inscriptions', in *The Indian Antiquary*, vol. vi, pp. 30–1. *Journal of the Bombay Branch of the Royal Asiatic Society*, vol. ix, no. xxvii, p. 229. *Epigraphia Indica*, vol. vii, App. no. 611 (p. 106).

IND. CH. 64

Three copper plates (22 × 6 cm.) held together by a thin, cut ring with a bulky oval seal (3 × 5 cm.). The plates are partly damaged by corrosion. The seal bears the inscriptions *Śrī Harivarmaṇā* and a swastika on both sides.

The text records the grant of the village of Maradē '. . . for use of holy people and for the purpose of the celebration of the rites of the temple which was the property of the sect of Śramaṇas called Ahariṣṭi and the authority of which was superintended by the *Ācārya* Dharmanandī . . .'. The grant was made at the request of king Bhānuśakti of the family of the Sēndrakas in the fifth regnal year of the Kadamba Harivarman.

J. F. Fleet, 'Sanskrit and Old-Canarese Inscriptions', in *The Indian Antiquary*, vol. vi, pp. 31–2. *Journal of the Bombay Branch of the Royal Asiatic Society*, vol. ix, no. xxvii, p. 229. *Epigraphia Indica*, vol. vii, App. no. 612 (p. 106).

IND. CH. 65

Five copper plates (23 × 9 cm.) held together by a copper ring with a circular seal (5 cm. diameter) showing, in relief, a standing elephant.

The language is a mixture of Sanskrit and Kannada; i.e. lines 1–33 are in Sanskrit, 34–53 in Kannada, 54–9 in Sanskrit, 60–2 in Kannada.

The grant was made by the Western Gaṅga king Rājamalla I in *Śaka-samvat* 750 (elapsed) (i.e. A.D. 829/30). The text describes how the village of Doḍḍavāḍi in the Manya district, was given to the Brahmin Dēva Śarman '. . . in order to provide for oblations, incense, and lamps for the goddess . . .'.

The plates were found at Manne, near Bangalore.

Rao Bahadur R. Narasimhachar, *Annual Report of the Archaeological Department of Mysore State*, 1909–10, p. 24.

IND. CH. 66

Two copper plates (40 × 31 cm.) with raised rims, two ring holes, and two seals. Both seals are of oval shape. The larger one (5 × 6 cm.) is well preserved and shows, in relief, a bull and an unintelligible inscription. The second seal is smaller and badly corroded. Neither seal is now physically attached to the plates but it can be assumed that at least one of the seals did originally belong to them.

The language of the grant is Sanskrit. The plates are inscribed on one side only. The text records how the village of Peḍhapatra was given to a Brahmin by Dhruvasēna III of Valabhī in *Samvat* 333 (i.e. A.D. 652).

IND. CH. 67

A miscellaneous collection of seven (incomplete) grants on nine copper plates.

Ind. Ch. 67. a. Three copper plates (29 × 20 cm.) with two ring holes. The plates are badly damaged by corrosion. The language is Sanskrit, the script *Grantha*. The plates give only the introductory portion of the grant referring to the lineage of some Vaiṣṇavite and Śaivite kings. The plates belong to the seventh or eighth century A.D. and, to all appearances, come from the same area as *Ind. Ch. 66.*

Ind. Ch. 67. b. One copper plate (30 × 22 cm.) without ring holes, badly damaged by corrosion. The language is Sanskrit, the script *Grantha* though slightly different in character to the one used on the above grant. The plate is part of a grant made in the eighth century A.D. apparently by a king named *Mahārāja* Bhutasimha.

Ind. Ch. 67. c. One copper plate (31 × 26 cm.) badly damaged by corrosion. The plate has two ring holes and forms part of an eighth-century grant. The language is Sanskrit, the script *Grantha.*

Ind. Ch. 67. d. One copper plate (34 × 25 cm.) with slightly raised rims badly damaged by corrosion. There are no ring holes. The language is Sanskrit, the script *Grantha.* The plate forms part of a grant belonging to the same time and place as *Ind. Ch. 67. a.*

Ind. Ch. 67. e. One copper plate (31 × 22 cm.) badly damaged by corrosion. The plate forms part of an eighth-century grant. There is one ring hole and one corner is reinforced by a piece of metal. The language is Sanskrit, the script *Grantha.*

Ind. Ch. 67. f. One copper plate (31 × 21 cm.) badly damaged by corrosion. One corner is missing. The plate is part of an eighth-century grant. The language is Sanskrit, the script *Grantha.*

Ind. Ch. 67. g. One copper plate (33 × 26 cm.) badly damaged by corrosion with a copper-plate reinforcement at the back. The plate forms part of an eighth-century grant. The language is Sanskrit, the script *Grantha.*

APPENDIX

THE British Museum owns one additional copper-plate grant which is kept in the Department of Oriental Antiquities and bears the number *1957, 11–12, 1*. The charter consists of one single plate inscribed on both sides with a seal depicting a ten-armed Śiva affixed to the top. The language is Sanskrit, and the script an early form of the Bengali alphabet. The grant was made by Vijayasēna of Bengal (*c.* A.D. 1095–1158). The copper plate was presented to the Museum by Captain Raymond Johnes.

Inscriptions of Bengal, vol. iii (1929), pp. 57–67. R. D. Banerji, 'Barrackpur Grant of Vijayasena: the 32nd Year', in *Epigraphia Indica*, vol. xv, pp. 278–86. R. G. Basak, *Sāhitya*, vol. xxxi (1328 B.S.), pp. 81 ff.

INDEX